D1709995

GEOLOGY GENIUS

SEDIMENTARY ROCKS

by Rebecca Pettiford

po§o

Ideas for Parents and Teachers

Pogo Books let children practice reading informational text while introducing them to nonfiction features such as headings, labels, sidebars, maps, and diagrams, as well as a table of contents, glossary, and index.

Carefully leveled text with a strong photo match offers early fluent readers the support they need to succeed.

Before Reading

- "Walk" through the book and point out the various nonfiction features. Ask the student what purpose each feature serves.
- Look at the glossary together. Read and discuss the words.

Read the Book

- Have the child read the book independently.
- Invite him or her to list questions that arise from reading.

After Reading

- Discuss the child's questions. Talk about how he or she might find answers to those questions.
- Prompt the child to think more. Ask: Have you ever visited a popular sedimentary rock formation like the Grand Canyon? Would you like to?

Pogo Books are published by Jump!
5357 Penn Avenue South
Minneapolis, MN 55419
www.jumplibrary.com

Library of Congress Cataloging-in-Publication Data

Names: Pettiford, Rebecca, author.
Title: Sedimentary rocks / by Rebecca Pettiford.
Description: Minneapolis, MN: Jump!, Inc., [2018]
Series: Geology genius | "Pogo Books are published by Jump!" | Audience: Ages 7-10.
Includes bibliographical references and index.
Identifiers: LCCN 2017059755 (print)
LCCN 2017059277 (ebook)
ISBN 9781624968471 (ebook)
ISBN 9781624968457 (hardcover: alk. paper)
ISBN 9781624968464 (pbk.)
Subjects: LCSH: Sedimentary rocks–Juvenile literature. Sedimentology–Juvenile literature.
Classification: LCC QE471 (print)
LCC QE471 .P41985 2018 (ebook) | DDC 552/.5–dc23
LC record available at https://lccn.loc.gov/2017059755

Editor: Kristine Spanier
Book Designer: Michelle Sonnek
Content Consultant: Sandra Feher, M.S.G.E.

Photo Credits: All photos by Shutterstock except: Gary Crabbe/Getty, 14-15; ullstein bild/Getty, 20-21.

Printed in the United States of America at Corporate Graphics in North Mankato, Minnesota.

TABLE OF CONTENTS

CHAPTER 1

LAYERS OF ROCK

Earth is more than 4.5 billion years old. Its rock is always changing. It breaks down. It forms again. This is the **rock cycle**.

sedimentary
rock

Earth has three types
of rock. **Igneous** and
metamorphic are two.
Sedimentary is the third.
What is it? Rock formed
by layers of **sediment**.

Sediment is broken rock fragments. What breaks rock? Wind. Water. Heat. Ice. It takes many years. **Weathering** and **erosion** affect sedimentary rock the most. The small bits end up in lakes, streams, and oceans. This is called **deposition**.

sediment

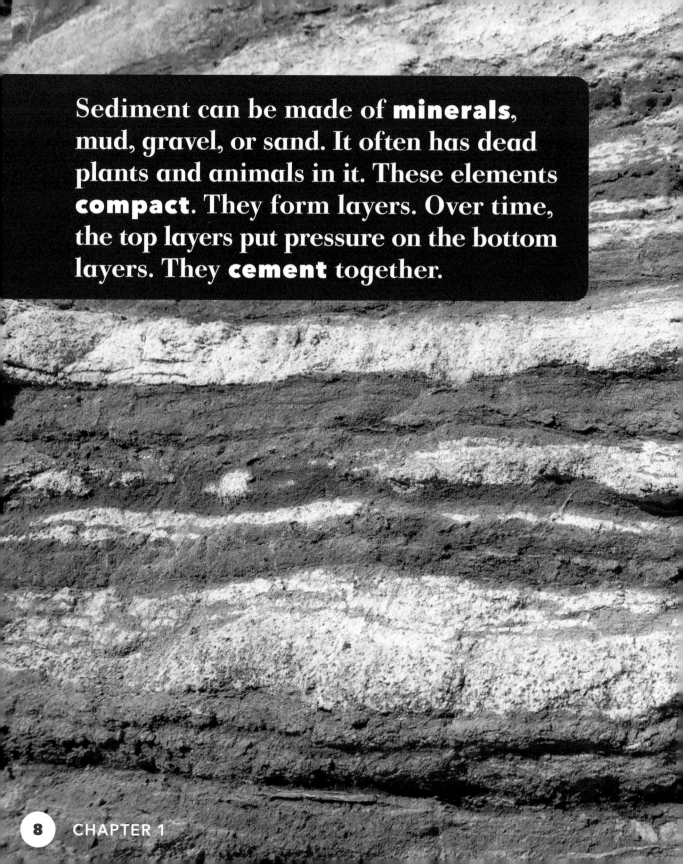

Sediment can be made of **minerals**, mud, gravel, or sand. It often has dead plants and animals in it. These elements **compact**. They form layers. Over time, the top layers put pressure on the bottom layers. They **cement** together.

TAKE A LOOK!

Sediment is often blown or washed into water. Over time, the layers form sedimentary rock.

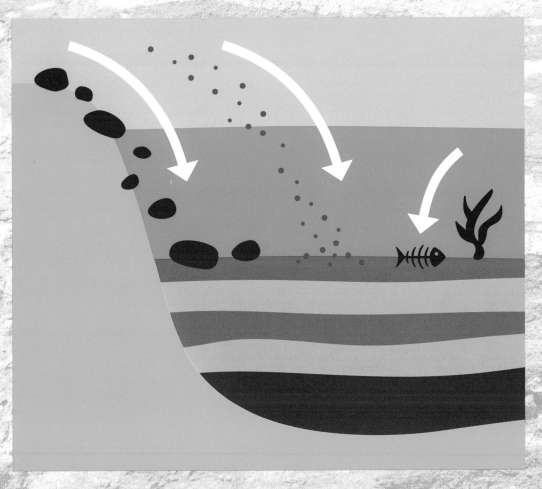

■ = land
■ = sea
■ = materials washed into sea
■ = materials blown into sea

■ = dead plants and animals
▨ = sediment layers
■ = sedimentary rock

fossil

Fossils are found in this rock. They tell scientists what kinds of plants and animals once lived in the area. We learn more about the history of Earth.

DID YOU KNOW?

Most fossils form in water. Why? This is where sediment is more likely to bury the plant or animal quickly.

CHAPTER 2

FABULOUS FORMATIONS

Wind and rain carved the Delicate Arch in Utah. It is made of red **sandstone**.

Delicate Arch ·····▸

The Wave

This is The Wave in Arizona. It formed more than 190 million years ago! Desert sands compacted. Minerals in water moving through the sand added color. Can you see the shapes that wind and water made?

Take a peek at Earth's crust in the Grand Canyon. The Colorado River carved the **canyon**. Layers of sediment have settled here for billions of years. Each layer is a different color. Buff. Gray. Green. Pink. Slate-gray. Brown. Violet. Layers at the bottom are more than 4 billion years old.

DID YOU KNOW?

The Grand Canyon is 277 miles (446 kilometers) across. It is more than one mile (1.6 km) deep in some areas.

Grand Canyon

Badlands
National Park

Badlands National Park is in South Dakota. Changes in **climate** can be seen here. Each change leaves a different layer of rock behind. The layers are made of grains of sand, silt, and clay. The bottom layer is the oldest. These formations continue to be sculpted. How? By weathering and erosion.

CHAPTER 3

ROCK AT WORK

How do we use sedimentary rock? We use **limestone** in buildings. The pyramids in Egypt are made of it!

pyramid

White House

Many buildings in the United States are made of it, too. Like what? The White House!

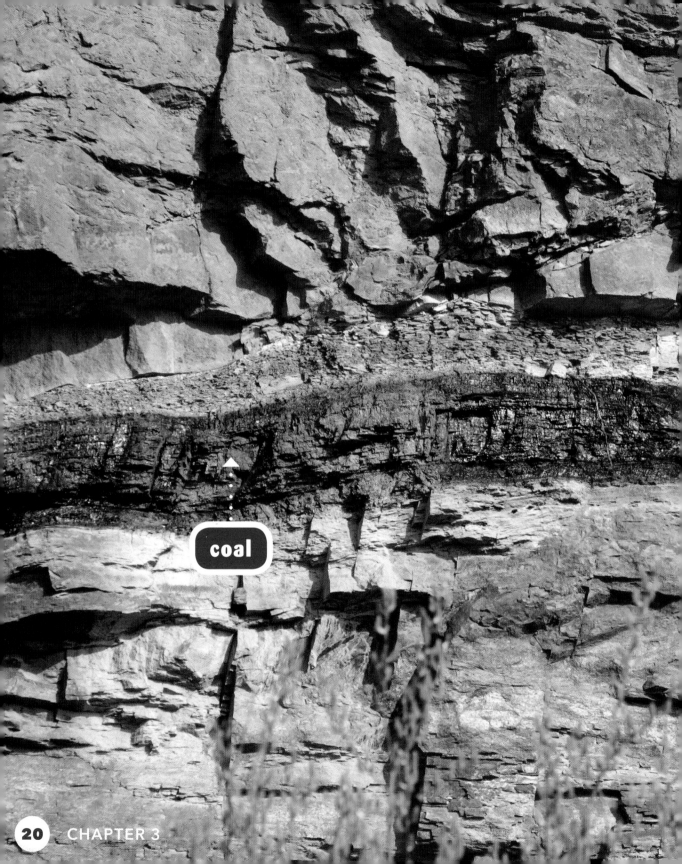

coal

Fossil fuels are found in sedimentary rock. What are they? Oil. Natural gas. Coal. They produce energy. We are able to heat our homes. Cook our food. Travel in cars.

Earth produces amazing rocks. They are important to our way of life!

DID YOU KNOW?

Fossil fuels form from the remains of plants and animals. The weight of sand and mud compact them. Heat from Earth helps transform them. We are using them faster than they can be replaced.

ACTIVITIES & TOOLS

MAKE SEDIMENTARY LAYERS

See how sedimentary layers form in rivers, lakes, and oceans.

What You Need:
- clean glass jar with a lid
- sand
- soil
- dead plant material (roots, leaves, stems)
- gravel
- water

1 Pour a layer of sand into the jar.

2 Add a layer of soil.

3 Add the dead plant material.

4 Add a layer of gravel.

5 Fill the jar ¾ full of water.

6 Screw on the lid. Shake the jar until everything is mixed together.

7 Set the jar down and let it sit. Look at it every day. Record the results over a week or two. What do you start to notice? You should see the materials settle to the bottom of the jar in different layers.

GLOSSARY

canyon: A deep river valley with steep sides.

cement: To bind together and hold in place.

climate: The weather typical of a certain place over a long period of time.

compact: To press or crush something together.

deposition: The process in which sediment is added to a landform or land mass.

erosion: To be worn away by water, wind, heat, or ice.

fossil fuels: Fuels like coal, oil, or natural gas that come from dead plants or animals.

fossils: The remains, traces, or prints of plants or animals from the past that are preserved in rock.

igneous: Rock made by cooled magma or lava that has hardened.

limestone: Rock formed from the remains of shells or coral.

metamorphic: Of or having to do with rock that has been formed by pressure and heat.

minerals: Solid, natural substances with crystal structures, usually obtained from the ground.

rock cycle: The continuous process by which rocks are created, changed from one form to another, destroyed, and then formed again.

sandstone: Rock made up mostly of sand-like grains of mineral, rock, or plant and animal materials.

sediment: Minerals, mud, gravel, or sand, or a combination of these, that have been carried to a place by water, wind, or glaciers.

weathering: The physical and chemical breakdown of materials at or near Earth's surface.

INDEX

TO LEARN MORE

Learning more is as easy as 1, 2, 3.

1) Go to www.factsurfer.com

2) Enter "sedimentaryrocks" into the search box.

3) Click the "Surf" button to see a list of websites.

With factsurfer, finding more information is just a click away.